Historical Biographies

MARCO POLO

Robert Strathloch

Heinemann Library
Chicago, Illinois

© 2002 Reed Educational and Professional Publishing Ltd
Published by Heinemann Library,
an imprint of Reed Educational & Professional Publishing,
Chicago, Illinois

Customer Service 888-454-2279
Visit our website at www.heinemannlibrary.com

Designed by Celia Floyd
Illustrated by Jeff Edwards and Joanna Brooker
Printed in Hong Kong

06 05 04 03 02
10 9 8 7 6 5 4 3 2 1

Library of Congress Cataloging-in-Publication Data
Strathloch, Robert, 1961-
  Marco Polo / Robert Strathloch.
      p. cm. -- (Historical biographies)
Summary: Presents an overview of Marco Polo's life as well as his influence on history and the world.
  ISBN: 1-58810-567-9 (HC), 1-4034-0147-0 (Pbk.)
  1. Polo, Marco, 1254-1323?--Juvenile literature. 2. Explorers--Italy--Biography--Juvenile literature. 3. Travel, Medieval--Juvenile literature. [1. Polo, Marco, 1254-1323?--Juvenile literature. 2. Explorers.] I. Title. II. Series.
  G370.P9 S77 2002
  910'.92--dc21

                            2001003662

Acknowledgments
The author and publishers are grateful to the following for permission to reproduce copyright material:
p. 4 Ancient Art and Architecture; p. 6 Wolfgang Kaehler/Corbis; pp. 7, 19 Bodleian Library; p. 8 Hulton Archive; pp. 9, 17, 27 Biblioteque National Paris; pp. 10, 18, 24, 28 The Art Archive; pp. 11, 23 Adam Woolfitt/Corbis; p. 12 Mary Evans Picture Library; p. 13 Adrian Arbib/Corbis; p. 14 Fotomas; p. 15 Corbis; p. 16 Roger Viollet; p. 21 Biblioteque National Paris/The Bridgeman Art Library; p. 25 Hulton Getty; p. 26 Werner Forman Archive; p. 29 Hereford Cathedral.

Special thanks to Rebecca Vickers for her comments in the preparation of this book.

Every effort has been made to contact copyright holders of any material reproduced in this book. Any omissions will be rectified in subsequent printings if notice is given to the publisher.

Some words are shown in bold, **like this.** You can find out what they mean by looking in the glossary.

Many Italian and Chinese names and terms may be found in the pronunciation guide.

Contents

Note to the reader:
Some of the dates in this book are not exact. History
was not always written down well during Marco Polo's
time. Many historians disagree on the exact dates for
events during this time period.

Who was Marco Polo?

Marco Polo was one of the world's greatest travelers. When he was just seventeen years old, he traveled from Italy all the way to China. He traveled in boats, on horses, and on camels. He made notes of everything he saw. When Marco returned to Italy 24 years later, he wrote a book about his travels.

Marco Polo's book became very popular. Mapmakers and **explorers** were excited by his descriptions of the gold, spices, and other riches in the cities of the East. Marco's stories made them dream of wealth and adventure. His stories also inspired many Europeans to go on **expeditions** to China and other places in the Far East.

Marco also brought back information about different people and **civilizations**. For the first time, Europeans could read about people and places that they knew very little or nothing about. Marco described mountains, deserts, and rivers. He wrote about the buildings, art, governments, religions, and **customs** that he had seen in different lands.

◄ **This illustration shows Marco as a young man. By the time he was twenty in 1274, he had traveled farther than most other Europeans.**

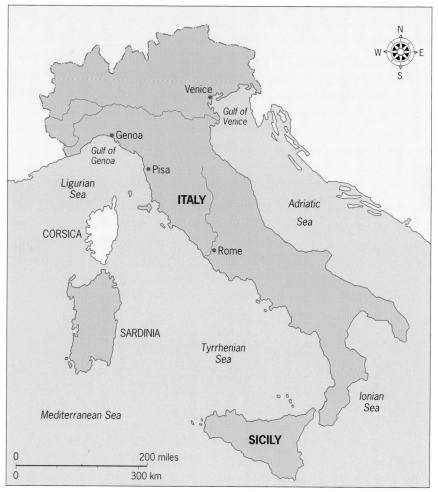

◀ Marco Polo spent the first years and last years of his life in Venice, Italy.

How do we know?

There is little information about Marco Polo's early childhood and later life. He was born and lived in the Italian city of Venice. Many letters and descriptions of life in Venice have survived from Marco's time. The main source of information about Marco's travels come from the book he wrote called *The Description of the World*. It is full of information about where he went and what he saw.

Key dates

1254	Birth of Marco Polo
1271	Marco, Niccolò, and Maffeo Polo leave Venice for China
1274	The Polos reach Shangdu and meet Kublai Khan
1292	The Polos leave China to return to Venice
1295	The Polos arrive back in Venice
1297	Marco Polo jailed in Genoa
1324	Death of Marco Polo

5

Marco Polo's Early Life

Marco Polo was born around 1254 in the Italian city of Venice. His father was a rich **merchant** named Niccolò Polo. Niccolò spent a lot of time away from home, traveling in foreign lands where he traded **goods** in faraway cities.

Marco's mother died when he was a young boy. At that time, Niccolò Polo and his brother, Maffeo were away on a **trading mission.** So, Marco was sent to live with an aunt and uncle. He would have started school from about age five or six. He probably had lessons in reading, writing, geography, and math. In addition, Marco also probably learned how to use foreign money, inspect products, and deal with **cargo** ships.

▲ **Many of the buildings from Marco's time are still in Venice today.**

Growing up in Venice

When Marco was growing up, Venice was a beautiful city. The city was built on many small islands. There were no streets between the houses. Instead there were **canals**, and people went everywhere in small boats. Along the canals were the houses and palaces of rich merchants and **noble** families. The city's **harbor** was crowded with trading ships from different parts of the world. Merchants brought beautiful **silks** from China, spices from Indonesia, precious stones from India, and **incense** from Arabia.

▲ This painting shows what Venice would have looked like when Marco Polo was alive.

La Serenissima

When Marco was growing up, Italy was not a united country as it is today. It was made up of many independent **city-states.** Venice had a trading **empire** that stretched around the Mediterranean Sea. People called Venice *La Serenissima* or "The Most Serene" because it was one of the richest and most powerful cities in Europe.

Setting Off to China

Marco's father returns

Marco's father Niccolò and uncle Maffeo Polo returned to Venice in 1269. They had been away for all of Marco's life. He was fifteen years old when they came back. It must have been strange for Marco to meet his father for the first time. He was probably fascinated, though, to hear about all the lands they had visited.

One of the lands Niccolò and Maffeo visited was China, known by Europeans at that time as Cathay. Niccolò and Maffeo had to avoid fighting armies in the Middle East. While trying to avoid the armies, they ended up in China. The brothers brought back **silks**, spices, and other **goods**. They also brought back a letter from the **emperor** of China, Kublai Khan. The letter asked the **Pope** to send 100 **Christian scholars** to China. Kublai Khan wanted to learn more about the Christian religion.

◄ Kublai Khan was the first **Mongol** emperor of China. He ruled China for 34 years, from 1260 to 1294.

A new journey to China

When Niccolò and Maffeo returned to Venice, the Pope had died. They decided to wait in Venice until a new Pope was elected. After two years they could wait no longer. In 1271, they prepared to leave for China. This time, they asked seventeen-year-old Marco to join them. In the summer of 1271, Niccolò, Maffeo, and Marco Polo sailed from Venice eastward across the Mediterranean Sea to the port of Acre (now Akko, Israel). There they learned that a new Pope had been elected. He sent two **friars** to accompany the Polos to China.

▲ This painting shows Niccolò, Maffeo, and Marco Polo leaving Venice for China in 1271.

The Tartars

In 1206, armies of **Tartars** moved out of their lands in northeast Asia, known today as Mongolia. A **warrior** named Genghis Khan led them. Within 50 years, they built an **empire** that stretched from China to eastern Europe. When Marco traveled to China, the **Great Khan** of the Mongols—as the Tartars became known—was Kublai Khan.

Strange Sights

From Acre, the Polos sailed northward up the eastern coast of the Mediterranean Sea to Ayas in present-day Turkey. This was an important trading port. Many **merchants** from Italy went there to buy **goods** from the East.

The friars leave

When they arrived in Ayas, the Polos heard that armies from Egypt were attacking the lands they were planning to cross. The two **friars** traveling with them were frightened when they heard this news. They refused to go any further and returned to Acre. The Polos were disappointed, but decided that they must continue their journey.

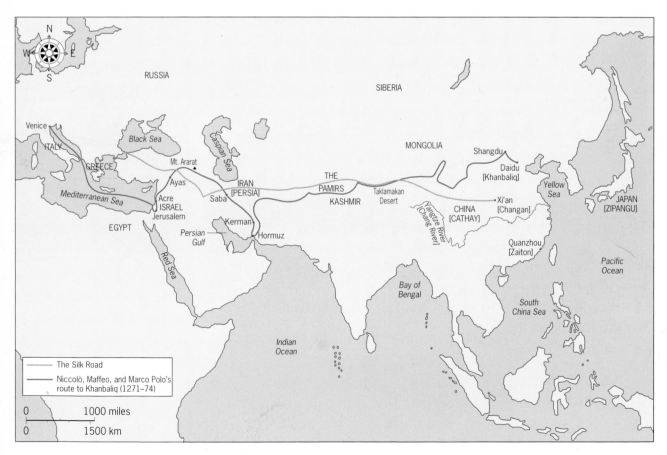

▲ This map shows the Polos' journey from Venice to China.
Their trip lasted three and a half years.

On to Kerman

The Polos now took a more northerly route to avoid the attacking Egyptian soldiers. This route took them inland into an area called Turkomania (now part of Turkey). At times they were only able to travel 10 miles (16 kilometers) a day because the roads were so bad.

As they traveled further away from Europe, Marco saw many new things. He took notes of everything he saw—the towns and cities they passed through, the mountains and rivers they crossed, and the people they met. They passed Mount Ararat where, according to the Bible, **Noah's Ark** was said to have landed after the Flood. In Persia (now Iran) they saw a fountain of oil that gushed out of the ground. They soon reached the Persian towns of Saba and then Kerman.

◄ Mount Ararat in modern Turkey was just one of the amazing sights the Polos saw on their journey to China.

Safety in numbers

Traveling overland in Marco's time could be very dangerous. Travelers were often attacked and robbed by **bandits**. The Polos and their servants tried to join larger merchant **caravans** whenever they could. A larger group would give them more protection from bandits.

Trouble on the Road

The Polos began heading south toward the Persian Gulf. They wanted to catch a boat there that would take them to China. Traveling by sea at that time could be very dangerous. Ships could be wrecked in storms or on rocks. Even with these dangers, sailing was still considered safer than traveling overland.

Bandits attack

From a valley near Kerman, the Polos entered an area filled with **bandits.** For safety, they had joined another **caravan** of **merchants.** As they entered the mountains, a dust storm suddenly blew over them and they were attacked. Many of the travelers were killed or captured. The Polos managed to escape and hide in a nearby village.

▲ Attacks by bandits were a continuous danger to merchants traveling along the **Silk** Road.

The journey continues overland

They traveled for a few more days until they reached the port of Hormuz on the Persian Gulf. Their plan was to join a trading ship that would be sailing around the coast of India to China. The Polos were shocked by what they saw in the **harbor**. All the ships looked old and damaged. Niccolò decided that even though the land route was dangerous, it would be better to continue their journey overland. Niccolò did not want to risk being shipwrecked in one of those boats. After a few days, the Polos joined another caravan heading eastward.

▲ Camel caravans like this one were common ways merchants transported their **goods** in Marco's time. In some places, people still use camel caravans.

The Silk Road

Most merchants during Marco's time traveled along a route made up of roads and tracks that became known as the Silk Road. A group of merchants would carry goods partway and then pass them to another group who would pass the goods to another. This created a system of trade from China to the Mediterranean Sea. The Polos followed the Silk Road, but unlike most merchants, they traveled all the way to China themselves.

The "Roof of the World"

The Polos traveled 200 miles (322 kilometers) back to Kerman. They had to pass through the same mountains where they had been attacked by **bandits**. They probably took soldiers to give them extra protection.

High into the mountains

After resting at Kerman, they continued their journey. The green fields surrounding the town slowly turned into desert sands. For days they traveled through this bare, hot region. Eventually they saw the peaks of the Pamir Mountains. These mountains were known as the "Roof of the World." The mountains are so high that their peaks are always covered in thick snow and ice.

▲ Marco saw many animals for the first time during his journey to China. This is the Marco Polo sheep, commonly found in the Pamirs.

It took the Polos twelve days to cross the Pamir Mountains. When they came down the other side they crossed into the green valleys of Kashgar. Marco thought that Kashgar was one of the most beautiful places he had ever seen.

Crossing a desert

From Kashgar they had to cross the Taklamakan Desert in northwest China. The Polos had little food and water. After 30 days, they finally made it to the other side. When they reached the town of Suchow, messengers sent by Kublai Khan met them. Their journey was almost over. They would soon meet the **Great Khan.**

▶ The green valleys of Kashgar look very much the same as when the Polos traveled through this area over 700 years ago.

Desert sights and sounds

As the Polos crossed the mountains and deserts, they heard whispering and singing. Travelers believed that these sounds could lead them off the trails and to their deaths. No one knew at that time that only winds and sands caused the noises. They also saw **mirages.** Mirages look like pools of water in the desert, but they are not really there.

15

Meeting the Great Khan

The city of Shangdu

The messengers traveled with the Polos for 40 days. In 1274, they arrived at Shangdu, where Kublai Khan had his summer palace. The Polos had been traveling for three and a half years. Now they would finally meet the great **emperor.** Marco was about 20 years old.

Kublai Khan held a great feast in honor of the Polos. He was about 60 years old at this time. Marco was impressed by Kublai Khan's appearance. He described Kublai Khan in great detail in his notebook. He was also amazed by the way the emperor lived, describing his summer palace in his notebook, too.

▲ This illustration shows what Kublai Khan's summer palace in Khanbaliq might have looked like.

The city of Daidu

When the summer was over, Kublai Khan invited the Polos to come to his capital city of Daidu (now modern Beijing). Daidu was larger than any city Marco had ever seen. It was full of large stone houses and broad, straight streets. Kublai Khan's palace was at the center of the city.

Marco saw many things he had never seen before while in Daidu. Courtyards and beautiful gardens surrounded many of the houses. People used paper money, unknown in Europe at that time. Coal, which was never used in Venice, was burned in fires. Marco was also impressed by the postal service. A network of riders on horseback came from all parts of China. They delivered official letters and government information to the emperor everyday.

▼ Niccolò and Maffeo Polo met Kublai Khan once before during their first trip to China. This picture shows their first meeting.

Dining in Style

Marco described what dining was like at Kublai Khan's palace in Daidu. The dining hall could seat 6,000 people. During dinner, magicians were said to have made golden cups fly through the air. These cups would land in the hands of the emperor without being touched by anyone else.

Working for Kublai Khan

As well as finding out all he could about Daidu and China, Marco was very eager to learn the languages of the East. The country was so large that many different languages were spoken. Marco began to learn four of the main languages.

Marco gets a job

The **Mongol Empire** was so huge that Kublai Khan could not possibly travel to every part himself. For years he had been looking for someone who would be able to travel, observing and reporting back on everything he saw. Marco's intelligence and travel experience impressed Kublai Khan. He sent Marco on journeys all over his empire. Marco worked for Kublai Khan for the next seventeen years.

▶ While traveling for Kublai Khan, Marco saw much of China's countryside.

Marco's first **expedition** was to the Chinese province of Yunnan. The journey took four months. He traveled as far as Tibet and Burma. All along the way Marco took notes about the land and **customs** of the people he saw. His second expedition was to the southeastern province of Mangi. Mangi was crossed by the Yangtze River (now the Chang River). It was so wide in places that it looked like a sea. At the end of each trip, Marco immediately returned to Daidu. He reported to Kublai Khan on what he saw. In this way, the **emperor** learned important information about his empire.

▼ During Marco's second expedition, he visited the city of Kinsai (now Hangzhou). At that time, Kinsai was a center of learning in China.

Outsiders welcome

Kublai Khan and other Mongol rulers liked using outsiders to work in their government. These *se mu*, or "colored eyes" ranked above the Chinese people who lived in the Mongol Empire. Mongols felt that they could not trust Chinese officials. Outsiders, like Marco Polo, would give them a more accurate opinion.

Beyond the Borders of China

Kublai Khan also sent Marco on **expeditions** outside China. The **emperor** was just as interested to find out about the lands outside his **empire** as he was to learn about his own territories.

A trip outside of China

In 1285, Marco boarded a wooden ship called a **junk** and set sail from the port of Zaiton (now Quanzhou) for India. His first stop was probably the island of Hainan. He then sailed to Java, the center of the spice trade. He visited Sumatra where he stayed for five months because of storms. Then he sailed to the Andaman Islands and Ceylon (now Sri Lanka). Marco described seeing beautiful deep-red **rubies** and bright blue **sapphires** there. In the city of Kandy he saw a tooth said to be from the mouth of **Buddha**.

▶ This map shows the places Marco traveled to while working for Kublai Khan.

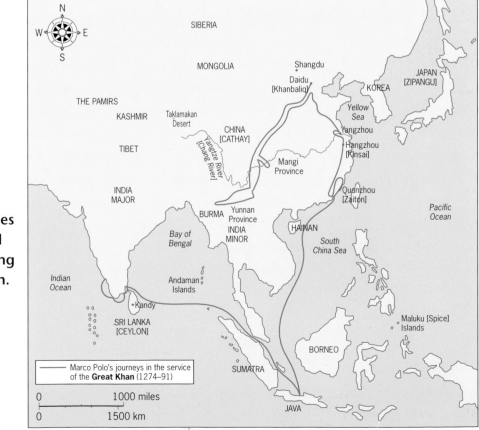

India

Marco sailed to the coast of India, which he thought was the richest and most beautiful country in the world. He saw men diving off boats to collect pearls from oysters off the sea floor. He spent many months traveling around the southern parts of India. Marco visited kings and queens and watched the religious festivals of **Hindu** priests.

Unusual Animals

Marco saw many animals he had never seen before. In Sumatra he saw a rhinoceros, which he thought was a unicorn. Marco also saw "men with tails," which were probably large monkeys. In Ceylon he saw enormous elephants that rulers rode around on in golden chairs.

▲ This is an illustration of some of the animals Marco described seeing on his travels.

The Journey Home

Marco was 37 years old and had spent seventeen years working for Kublai Khan. He had become rich from his work for the **emperor** and his own trading work. Marco's father and uncle had continued their work as **merchants** and had also become rich. However, they wanted to return to Venice.

The Polos leave China

The Polos had to get Kublai Khan's permission to leave his **empire**. He did not want to see the Polos go, but sometime around 1292, he finally gave them permission to leave. The Polos set sail from the port of Zaiton. They were traveling with one of the royal princesses. She was leaving to marry a prince in Persia.

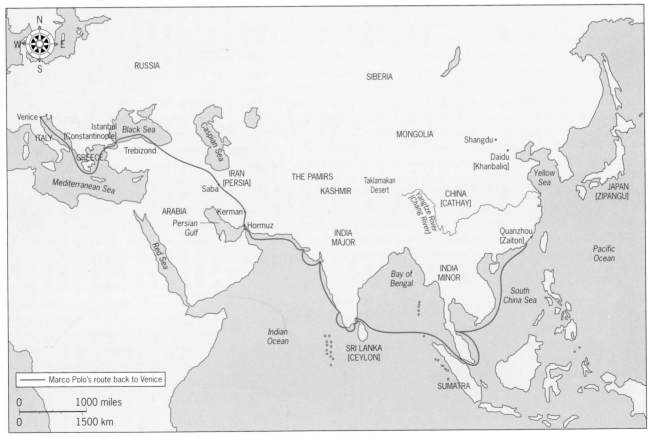

▲ This map shows the Polos' journey from China back to Venice. They had spent around seventeen years in China.

► A stone gate is all that remains of the Polos' house. This is where they knocked on the door, to the surprise of their family.

The weather was so bad that it took two years to reach the port of Hormuz. This journey would usually have taken about two months. The Polos traveled inland with the princess to Kerman. During this time they received news from Daidu that Kublai Khan had died. He was about 80 years old.

On to Venice

With new horses and supplies, the Polos continued on their journey home. They reached the port of Trebizond on the Black Sea. While there, they had many of their riches stolen. They sailed to Constantinople (now Istanbul, Turkey) and then sailed north to Venice. Marco, Niccolò, and Maffeo Polo finally arrived in Venice in 1295.

Strangers at the door

The Polos had been away for 24 years. Their family thought they were dead. When they knocked on the door of their house, their family hardly recognized them. It is said that they tore off their ragged coats, revealing **rubies**, diamonds, and emeralds. After that, their family believed they were who they said they were!

Marco Polo's Later Life

It must have been strange for Marco when he returned to Venice. He left the city in 1271 and returned in 1295. In the 24 years between, he had traveled to more lands than any European had ever done before.

Venice and Genoa: the fight for trade

Little is known of Marco's later life. While he had kept a record of his journeys to and from China and of his **expeditions**, little information exists of his life back in Venice. Marco did spend some time in prison. This happened in 1297. The two north Italian cities of Venice and Genoa were often fighting each other for control of the rich trade that entered Europe from the East. In that year, Marco was captured by the Genoans, possibly while commanding one of the Venetian warships at the sea

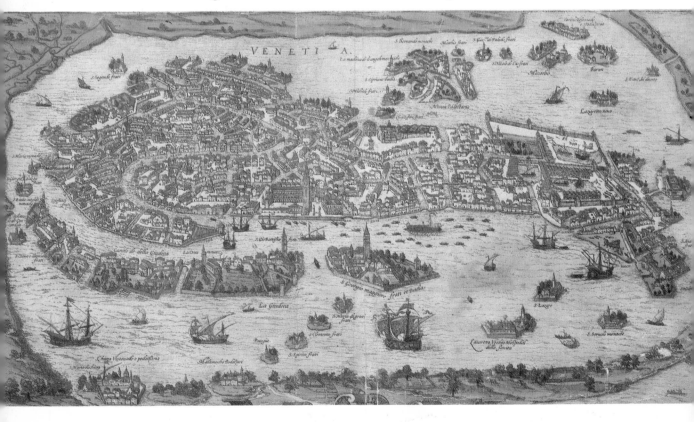

▲ The Polos' house was one of many along the Grand **Canal,** as seen in this old map of Venice.

battle of Curzola. With hundreds of others, he was taken to Genoa and thrown into prison.

Marco meets Rustichello

Marco's stories about his travels might never have been known had it not been for this event. In Genoa, he shared a prison cell with another man named Rustichello of Pisa. To pass time in their cell, Marco began to tell Rustichello about his exciting life. Rustichello was inspired by what he heard and started to write down the stories as Marco told them.

▶ This illustration shows Rustichello taking notes while Marco retells stories of his travels. They passed much of their time in prison this way.

Rustichello of Pisa

Rustichello was from the Italian town of Pisa. He was already a well-known writer when he met Marco. He wrote love stories, a popular subject at that time. Rustichello probably added his own style when writing out Marco's stories. He probably felt the need to make some of Marco's stories more "exciting."

Marco Polo's Final Years

Marco's stories become a book

In 1299, Venice and Genoa made peace. Marco was released from prison and allowed to return home. Soon after he returned to Venice, Marco had his stories that were written down by Rustichello made into a book. It is known today as *The Description of the World*. The book became popular and helped to increase European knowledge and interest in the East.

Life returns to normal

Marco became a **merchant** like his father and uncle. He never traveled as far away as he once did. He only went on short **trading missions** around the Mediterranean Sea. Sometimes Marco went to northern Europe and Russia, too.

Little information exists about Marco's later life. The Polo family bought several houses near the Grand **Canal** in Venice. When Marco was about 45 years old, he married a rich Venetian woman named Donata Badoer. They had three daughters. Marco Polo died at home in 1324 at the age of 70.

▶ This statue shows Marco holding a pomegranate. In Marco's time, this fruit was a symbol of wealth and success.

Marco's last words

A famous story states that as Marco lay dying, his friends asked him to admit the stories in his book were untrue. Marco is said to have supported the descriptions in his book until the day he died. He replied to his friends that he did not write half of what he saw.

▶ In his will (right), Marco left his few belongings to his wife and daughters. He also set free a **Mongol** slave who had traveled to Italy with him.

150 Descriptions of the World?

There are about 150 different versions of Marco's book, *The Description of the World*. His book came out before the invention of the printing press. So, people copied books by hand. These people would often add or remove information. No one usually cared about what the original text stated.

After Marco Polo

Marco Polo was the first European to write about his travels to China and all the things that he saw along the way. Marco was also one of the last European travelers to China for the next 500 years. Less than 100 years after his death, the new rulers of China decided that they did not want as much contact with the West. They closed China's borders to most travelers from the West.

The Description of the World is one of the most important and famous books ever written. It is important because it contains information about a world that was unknown to Europeans at that time. It is also a description of the **Mongol Empire** and the lands of the East. For over 500 years, it was the only record of an amazing period of contact between East and West.

◀ This painting shows Marco Polo during his later life.

MARCVS POLVS

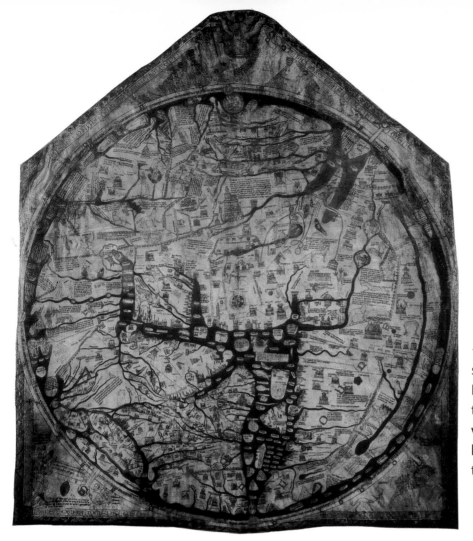

◄ This map shows what Europeans thought the world looked like before Marco's travels.

Marco Polo's book was one of the main sources of information about the East from the early 1400s until the late 1800s. Two hundred years after it was first written, *The Description of the World* encouraged Christopher Columbus to search for a sea route to China. His journey ended with the European settlement of North America. Today, Marco's stories still inspire people to take journeys of discovery and to visit many of the places he traveled to long ago.

Il Milione

In his book, Marco often described the things he saw in the Mongol Empire by the millions. Readers thought he must be lying. So, he was given the nickname *Il Milione* ("Million"). As more people visited the places Marco had described, **scholars** accepted that most of his stories really were true. Some people still believe that Marco did not visit all the places he described.

Glossary

bandit person who does not obey the law; robber

Buddha religious leader who lived in northern India over 2,000 years ago. People who believe in Buddha's teachings are called Buddhists.

canal man-made waterway for boats or land irrigation

caravan group of merchants or traders traveling overland together

cargo goods carried in a ship, airplane, or other vehicle

Christian person who believes in the teachings of Jesus Christ

city-state independent city and its surrounding territories that has its own ruler

civilization large group of people who have settled in one place and live in the same organized way, following the same rules and creating their own style of art

custom something that has been done for a long time and is accepted as a way of life

emperor chief ruler of an empire

empire group of territories or peoples under the same ruler

expedition journey to a place to find out what is there

explorer person who travels just to see what is there

friar Christian holy man who lives a simple life of teaching and prayer

good something produced for sale

Great Khan name given to the leader of the Mongol Empire

harbor safe place for boats and ships to stay

Hindu follower of the religion of Hinduism. Hinduism has many different branches, but believes in one universal spirit. It is the main religion of India.

incense substance that produces a sweet or spicy smell when burned

junk wooden sailing ship with square sails and a flat bottom used around China

merchant person who buys and sells goods for money

mirage illusion sometimes seen at sea, in the desert, or over hot pavement that looks like a pool of water or a mirror in which distant objects are seen

Mongol person from Mongolia; in Marco Polo's time, a person from northeast Asia

Noah's Ark according to the Bible, a large wooden ship built by a man named Noah in which he saved himself, his family, and living creatures of every kind during a world-wide flood

noble person of high birth or rank

Pope leader of the Roman Catholic Church

ruby very valuable stone that is used in jewelry. It is deep red in color.

sapphire very valuable stone that is used in jewelry. It is usually deep blue in color.

scholar person who has done advanced study in one or more subjects

silk cloth that is woven from the fibers produced by silkworms

Tartar old name for the Mongols

trading mission trip in which merchants go to buy and sell goods

warrior person involved or experienced in fighting

Time Line

1254	Marco Polo is born
1260	Kublai Khan elected **Great Khan** of China
1269	Niccolò and Maffeo Polo return to Venice from China
1271	Marco, Niccolò, and Maffeo Polo leave Venice for China
1274	The Polos arrive in China and meet Kublai Khan
1292	The Polos leave China for Venice
1294	Kublai Khan dies
1295	The Polos arrive in Venice
1297	Marco is imprisoned in Genoa
1298	Rustichello finishes writing Marco's stories
1299	Marco is released from prison
1299	*The Description of the World* is made into a book
1299	Marco marries Donata Badoer
1324	Marco Polo dies

Pronunciation Guide

Word	You say
Daidu	di-DOO
Il Milione	eel mee-lee-OH-nay
Khanbaliq	kaan-BA-leek
Kinsai	KIN-sigh
Kublai Khan	koo-BLA kaan
La Serenissima	la say-ra-NEE-see-ma
Mangi	man-GEE
Shangdu	shang-DOO
Yunnan	YOU-nan
Zaiton	ZAY-taan

More Books to Read

Ganeri, Anita. *Marco Polo*. Morristown, NJ: Silver Burdett Press, 1999.

Reid, Struan. *Marco Polo*. Chicago: Heinemann Library, 2001.
   An older reader can help you with this book.

Shuter, Jane. *The Middle Ages*. Chicago: Heinemann Library, 2001.

Index